INTRODUCTION

Welcome to the unique world of marriage, where love, laughter, tears and sadness unite in a sacred union called marriage. In this lighthearted exploration, be prepared to laugh from each illustration that depicts a true story.

Cute and unique. This is what describes marriage as a life adventure that can never be predicted. From small things to big things. The book "Funny Facts About Marriage" is your ticket to discovering the funny side of marital bliss. So, fasten your seat belts and get ready to laugh your way through heartwarming and side-splitting moments depicting hilarious married life.

Finally, please provide a review of this book as our motivation to make even more interesting books. Remember, maintaining the best health starts by laughing. Happy reading.

Robbert Piontek

TABLE OF CONTENTS

CHAPTER 1

"Being married is wonderful. Finding someone you want to bother for the rest of your life is amazing."

CHAPTER 2

"My wife says I never listen to her. At least I think that's what she said."

CHAPTER 3

"Marriage is a relationship where one person is always right, and the other person is the husband."

CHAPTER 4

"Marriage is when a man and woman promise to go through life together, hand in hand, and then start discussing whose hand gets the remote."

CHAPTER 5

"Maintaining mystery is essential to a happy marriage. For example, my wife doesn't realize that I forgot to bring her a anniversary present."

CHAPTER 6

"Getting married is wonderful, but what about divorce? Yes, that is a minimum of ten thousand dollars."

CHAPTER 7

"Compromise is the foundation of marriage. For instance, my wife makes concessions by allowing me to feel as though I'm in charge."

CHAPTER 8

"My wife advised me to accept the faults I've made. I then hugged her."

CHAPTER 9

"My wife admitted to fantasizing about me when I asked. She fantasized about me doing the laundry, cleaning the dishes, and taking out the trash."

CHAPTER 10

"Behind every successful man, there is a woman rolling her eyes."

CHAPTER 11

"Marriage is like a roller coaster. It has its ups and downs, and occasionally someone throws up."

CHAPTER 12

"Marriage is the bond between a person who never remembers their anniversary and another who never forgets them."

CHAPTER 13

"A deck of cards and marriage are similar. You only need a diamond and two hearts at first. By the end, all you need are an alibi and a shovel."

CHAPTER 14

"The secret to a happy marriage remains a secret because nobody has been able to find it"

CHAPTER 15

"Marriage is the only war where someone sleeps with the enemy"

CHAPTER 16

"The key to a successful marriage is a sense of humor and a long memory. So, you can laugh at the same mistakes over and over again"

CHAPTER 17

Being married is more than just a spiritual bond. And they remember who's supposed to take out the garbage."

CHAPTER 18

"A marriage is like to using a public restroom. People inside are wanting to go, while those outside are racing to get in."

CHAPTER 19

"A computer and a marriage are similar. The door could not open for you if you type the password incorrectly."

CHAPTER 20

"Driving a car and getting married are similar. You are in the wrong seat if you are not in control."

CHAPTER 21

"A marriage works similarly to a GPS. Even if it indicates that you've arrived, you could still be lost."

CHAPTER 22

"Marriage is like a smartphone. It's a great connection until someone forgets to charge it"

CHAPTER 23

"A marriage is like to a paid membership. It's all fresh and thrilling at first, but eventually you begin to wonder if you truly need it."

CHAPTER 24

"Marriage is when a man and a woman have different definitions of "five more minutes"

CHAPTER 25

"A marriage and a smartphone app are similar. To keep everything functioning properly, you occasionally need to restart and install updates."

CHAPTER 26

"A virtual meeting is what marriage is like. The mute button is there for a purpose, particularly in contentious situations."

CHAPTER 27

"A comedy film is what marriage is like. There are many humorous moments, surprising story turns, and occasional line-forgetting moments."

CHAPTER 28

"Marriage is like a car ride. Sometimes you navigate smoothly, and other times you get stuck in traffic without realizing it"

CHAPTER 29

"Marriage is like a team of superheroes. You both have unique strengths, occasional clashes, and the power to conquer each other"

CHAPTER 30

"Marriage is like a shopping receipt containing a list of mistakes made. At least that's what a husband thinks"

CHAPTER 31

"Marriage is like a labyrinth. It doesn't have straight way. No one knows the right way"

CHAPTER 32

"Marriage is when a baby was crying and there's only one person who wakes up the quickest."

CHAPTER 33

"In marriage there are only 2 rules. firstly, women are always right and secondly, if women made a mistake, remember the first rule"

CHAPTER 34

"Marriage is always faced with the choice of who follows whom."

CHAPTER 35

"Marriage is always faced with the choice of who is to blame."

CHAPTER 36

"It feels so good to be able to blame someone else."

CHAPTER 37

"Marriage is when someone says they want to go on a diet but orders pizza while their partner is at work."

CHAPTER 38

"Marriage is when someone says I am a reliable person but always forgets where to put the car keys."

CHAPTER 39

"Marriage is when someone says I love you but forgets what their promise was."

CHAPTER 40

"Marriage is when someone tells another person that their partner doesn't love them anymore just because they can't afford a luxury car

CHAPTER 41

"Marriage is when someone says I love you but installs an online dating app."

CHAPTER 42

"Marriage is when someone says I love you but is too lazy to go home right away."

CHAPTER 43

43

"Marriage is when someone says I love you but likes to imagine intimacy with someone else."

CHAPTER 44

44

"Marriage is when someone behaves differently compared to when they were dating."

CHAPTER 45

"Marriage is when someone holds their partner's hand and immediately releases their hand when they meet someone else."

CHAPTER 46

"Marriage is when someone makes a choice between material things and their partner."

CHAPTER 47

"Marriage is when someone feels like they contribute more than their partner."

CHAPTER 48

"Marriage is when someone tells other people about their partner's bad things."

CHAPTER 49

"Marriage is when someone forgets the marriage vows that were previously made."

CHAPTER 50

"Marriage is when someone thinks about their hobbies more than their partner."

CHAPTER 51

"Marriage is when someone thinks about the beauty of their body more than their partner."

CHAPTER 52

"Marriage is when someone says I love you but doesn't care what their partner says."

CHAPTER 53

"Marriage is when they say I love you but often break their promises."

CHAPTER 54

"Marriage is when they say I love you but they don't struggle to maintain their relationship when problems come."

CHAPTER 55

Marriage is when someone says I love you but often compares their partner to other people

CHAPTER 56

"Marriage is about teamwork, not individuals. but they didn't notice that'"

CHAPTER 57

57

"Marriage is when someone prefers to talk for a long time with another person than with their own partner."

CHAPTER 58

"Marriage is when they compare gifts from their partner with gifts from other people on their birthday."

CHAPTER 59

"Marriage is when a man still gives flowers and says I love you to his partner on their 5th wedding anniversary. it's just a myth."

CHAPTER 60

"Marriage is when a man still smiles when he sees his wife far away. but in reality they smile with other people."

CHAPTER 61

"Marriage is when someone panics because they don't know where their partner is. but in reality they feel more free"

CHAPTER 62

"Marriage is a time when they understand their respective roles in the household. It needs (brains)"

CHAPTER 63

"Marriage is when they can still laugh together after 25 years of marriage. Don't believe this. It is just a myth"

CHAPTER 64

"Marriage is when they still keep their marriage vows after 25 years of marriage. Trust me, It is a myth also"

CHAPTER 65

"Marriage is about those who help each other and do not blame each other. Can you? "

CHAPTER 66

"Marriage is those who still act like children and laugh together and laugh at each other's stupidity without making their partner hurt. Do you believe this?"

CHAPTER 67

"Marriage is like living on a ship. There is only one captain, the others just follow and give suggestions. but you know the facts , right ?"

CHAPTER 68

Marriage is like a bolt and a nut. They need each other but many times the nut want to become the bolt. That is when the problem comes. "

CHAPTER 69

There is no word "I" or "me" in a marriage. There are only two words that must always be thought of, namely "we/us. Remember that"

CHAPTER 70

"Marriage is making an effort to understand your partner's perspective and express your thoughts and feelings clearly."

CHAPTER 71

"Marriage is spending quality time together regularly. This could be through date nights, shared hobbies, or even just meaningful conversations.".

CHAPTER 72

"Marriage is showing respect for your partner's opinions, choices, and boundaries. Treat each other with kindness and consideration, even in moments of disagreement."

CHAPTER 73

"Marriage is giving each other space to pursue personal goals and passions.

CHAPTER 74

"Marriage is a journey with ups and downs. Be patient and understanding during challenging times. Work together to find solutions rather than blaming each other."

CHAPTER 75

"Marriage is ensuring that you and your partner have shared long-term goals and values. Common values provide a strong foundation for a lasting and meaningful connection."

CHAPTER 76

"Mistakes happen. Learn to forgive and let go of past grievances. Holding onto resentment can damage the relationship over time"

CHAPTER 77

"Life is unpredictable, and challenges are inevitable. Be flexible and adaptable in navigating the twists and turns together. A resilient attitude can strengthen your marriage"

CHAPTER 78

"Marriage is expressing gratitude and appreciation for your partner. Small gestures of kindness and acknowledgment go a long way in fostering a positive atmosphere in the relationship."

CONCLUSION

No husband and wife can be compatible from the moment they start. They are successful because they try together to understand each other and adapt to their partner's character. They support each other for every problem they face.

Marriage requires two reliable people. This is a team effort, not an individual effort. If you are currently having household problems, remember that storms don't happen every day. The storm will pass, but of course, it must be accompanied by joint efforts and intensive communication. If you have successfully lived your married life, share your life story with other people to encourage those who are still in the labyrinth

Thank you for reading this book. If you feel that this book is useful, I hope you are willing to spend your time providing a review of this book and sharing information about this book with people around you.

Best Wishes,

Robbert Piontek

See you again